A New Hat For Mommy

Helping children express
their concerns on cancer

Written and Illustrated by
Hannah Grace Perry

In the loving memory of:

My grandfather- Denis Johnson
Friends Ralph Grantham and his
daughter Catherine.

Dedicated to:

Casey Kaplan, Christine Jacqueline, Gerald
Brennan, Judith Abilock Clemmons, Ivan
and Patricia Green.

My name is Lucy and I am nine years old. I live in a big white house with my mommy, daddy and best friend Rose. Rose is my toy kitten. She is very important to me because I tell her all about the way I feel.

My mommy has to spend a lot of time in the hospital. She has a disease called cancer.

Every night Rose and I look out of our bedroom window and search for a star. We make a special wish for mommy. Rose tells me that making special wishes is a good idea.

Do you know what Lucy's wish might be?

It is cold tonight and I am in bed with Rose. Daddy reads us a goodnight story. He tells us we are going to see mommy tomorrow. I feel excited and a little scared. Rose tells me its okay to feel scared.

Why do you think Lucy might feel scared?

In the morning before I go to the hospital, I draw a picture for mommy. I know it will cheer her up and make her think of us together again. On the way to the hospital my tummy begins to ache. I think I am getting nervous. Rose tells me it is okay to feel nervous.

Why do you think Lucy is getting nervous?

Daddy and I peep through the window and notice mommy is looking different. She looks sad. That makes me feel down.

Daddy opens the door and I surprise her with my drawing. The nurse hangs the picture on the wall right next to mommy's bed so she can look at it whenever she wants. I am feeling very sad that mommy can't do all the things we used to do at home. Rose tells me it is okay to feel worried.

What things do you think mommy cannot do now?

Dr. Lewis comes in to visit mom and tells her what will be happening tomorrow. I really don't understand what the big words mean so Nurse Laura explains things to me.

Mommy will be having chemotherapy. It will help her cancer go away. Chemotherapy is a very strong medicine and so mommy is going to feel very tired and sick for a few days. It will also make her hair fall out. I feel very worried for mommy and I start to cry. I don't like what the nurse has told me. Rose told me it is okay to feel worried.

What do you think worries Lucy the most?

In bed that night daddy talks to me and Rose about mommy's hair falling out. Daddy told us that it isn't a bad thing, it just means that the medicine is working. Her hair will grow back, but very slowly, just like a baby's. I am okay with mommy not having hair, but Rose is wondering if it hurts when it falls out?

He said it won't hurt and that mommy won't even notice. She is going to feel very sick so we won't be able to visit for a few days. It is going to be our job to cheer her up again.

What kinds of things might cheer mommy up?

That night I couldn't sleep. I kept on thinking about all the things that might happen to mommy while she is in the hospital. I get frightened and begin to cry. Rose tells me it is okay to feel frightened.

Daddy comes in and hugs me. He sings our favorite song that mommy always sings at bedtime. This makes me feel better and I am able to fall asleep.

Does your mommy or daddy sing to you or read you a special story at bedtime?

In the morning daddy gives me a gift. It is a picture of mommy. I am very happy and put it by my bed. On the way to the hospital, Rose and I notice that the weather is warmer and we don't need hats and gloves today. I realize mommy has been in and out of the hospital for a long time. This makes me feel lonely.

Do you think that Lucy is alone?

At the hospital we all stop off at the gift shop and decide to buy mommy a special hat. I don't want mommy to feel bad that she has no hair. I pick out the baseball cap with a picture of a cat on it because it reminds me of Rose. It has pink on it, that is mommy's favorite color. Before we go into the room Dr. Lewis tells us we have to wear a face mask so that mommy does not catch any bad germs. I feel very afraid that I will get mommy sick and don't want to go into the room. The Doctor assures me everything is going to be okay.

I run in and hug mommy very carefully and give her the hat. She loves it and puts it on right away.

After a while I get thirsty and leave the room to get a drink. I see that there is a little girl waiting outside the room next door. I look through the window and notice that there is a man in the bed. I ask the little girl why she is crying and she tells me that her daddy is very sick.

I tell her about my mommy. The doctors and nurses are very good here and I think that they are going to take great care of our parents.

I put my arm around the little girl. I know that sometimes a hug can help me feel better.

Lucy realizes she really is not alone. As she walks down the hallway, she notices all kinds of people in their rooms. There are people who are young and old. There are moms and dads. There are a lot of doctors and nurses and everyone is very helpful. Lucy realizes that mommy is in the best place to get better.

Later on when we got home, I was excited to hear what story daddy would tell me. Every night daddy tells me all about when I was a baby and all the things that mommy would do with me. Story time is special to me and I look forward to it each day.

Do you like to hear stories of when you were little?

That night in bed I hugged Rose tight and thanked her for always being a good listener. I liked being able to tell Rose how I am feeling.

Why do you think Lucy likes to talk to Rose?

The next morning when I woke up, grandma was there. At first I was worried, but then I asked where daddy was. Grandma told me he had to pick up something very important and it couldn't wait.

After about an hour the doorbell rang and I ran to see if it was daddy. Grandma opened the door. I couldn't believe my eyes.
It was mommy. I was so happy I began to cry.

Do you think that Lucy was excited about mommy coming home? Do you think she might also be afraid?

Over the next few weeks Lucy went through lots of feelings. Somedays she would feel sad, other days happy. Somedays she would cry when people stared at her mommy's hair. It was really hard for her. Sometimes she had a lot of questions, but mommy or daddy would always try to answer them. This made Lucy feel better. Knowing what was going on stopped her from feeling so afraid.

Do you think that asking questions is a good idea?

Everyday that Lucy spends with her mommy, she feels blessed. She knows that not everyone gets to go home from the hospital. This does worry her. Rose has told Lucy that she should just be happy that mommy is in remission. This means that the cancer has gone away now. Lucy knows that it could come back, but right now, it's gone. Rose told Lucy she should stop worrying. It doesn't change things, so just enjoy today and every moment that you get to spend with the people that you love.

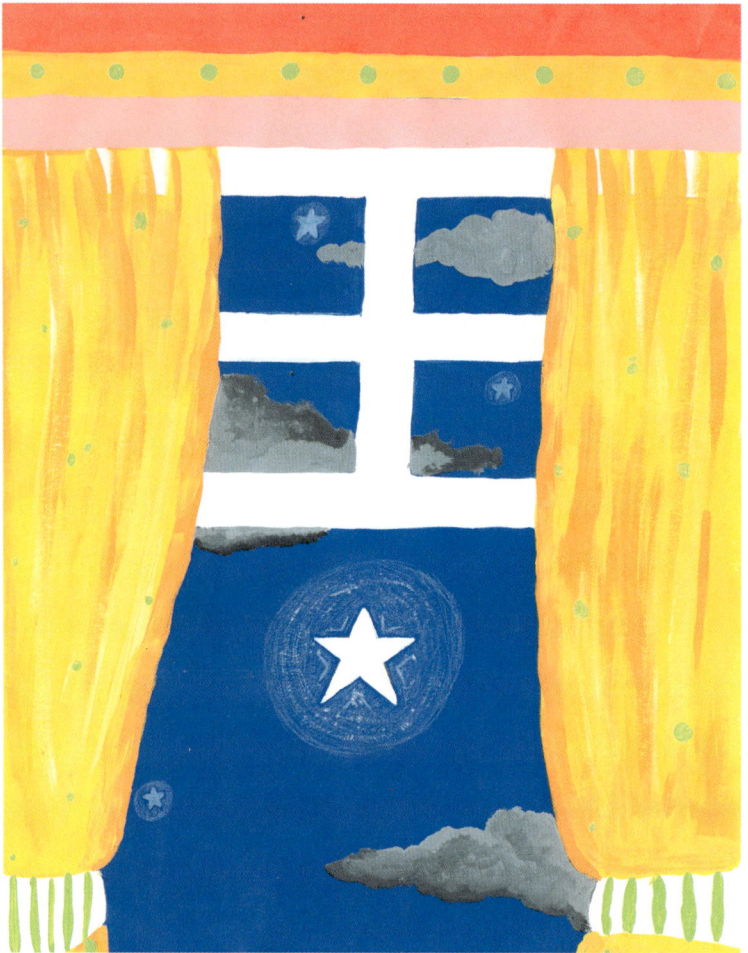

That night as Rose and Lucy listened to mommy singing their favorite song, they looked out the bedroom window and found a star. This time they didn't make a wish, they just said "Thank you."

THE END.

Written and Illustrated By Hannah Grace Perry.

With special thanks to:

My dear son- Harrison, and the few amazing friends that I have. Thank you for your constant love and encouragement over the years. You know who you are, and so do I!

Made in the USA
Las Vegas, NV
19 January 2021